NEWCOMER

PHONICS

Kaye Wiley

Longman

Pronunciation Key: Letter—Sound Relationships

Vowel Sounds

/a/ Nan, Tab, cat

/ā/ Kate, rain, play, great

/ä/ father, walk

/är/ car, farm

/ār/ chair

/e/ Bev, head

/ē/ Pete, see, me, read, monkey, baby, near, here, deer

/ėr/ her, girl, nurse

/i/ Tim, sit

/ī/ Mike, pie, my, night, Hi, fire, ice

/o/ Bob, dog,

/ō/ Rose, old, boat, no, slow, corn, door, scoreboard, four

/ô/ song, draw

/oi/ noise, toys

/ou/ cow, loud,

/u/ Gus, sun

/ù/ book, put

/ü/ Sue, flute, food, soup, juice

/ū/ music, few

/ə/ the, around, pencil

Consonant Sounds

/b/ bag

/d/ dog

/f/ fat, phone, gift

/g/ goat

/h/ hop

/j/ jog, cage

/k/ rock, Kate, cat, clock

/ks/ socks, box

/kw/ quiz, quack

/l/ lamp, class, plant, milk, hill

/m/ mat, jump, swimming

/n/ not, sand, tennis, know

/p/ pot, happy

/r/ run, grass, frog, write

/s/ swim, fast, face, dress

/t/ take, mitt

/v/ van

/w/ wait

/y/ yes

/z/ zoo, jogs

/ch/ chicken, beach, watch

/sh/ ship, fish

/th/ thin, with

/th/ the, this, that

/hw/ what, when, where

/ng/ sing

The following irregular words are not pronounced the way they are spelled. Each irregular word is listed below with a respelling to help you pronounce it.

above (əbuv), *ball* (bôl), *bananas* (bənanəz), *bounce* (bouns), *cheese* (chēz), *clothes* (klōz), *comes* (kumz), *do* (dü), *doll* (dol), *don't* (dōnt), *door* (dōr), *eight* (āt), *eyes* (īz), *face* (fās), *four* (fōr), *gone* (gôn), *great* (grāt), *has* (haz), *have* (hav), *hey* (hā), *huge* (hūj), *ice* (īs), *is* (iz), *isn't* (izənt), *juice* (jüs), *little* (litəl), *lives* (livz), *many* (menē), *minutes* (minits), *of* (əv), *off* (ôf), *one* (wun), *page* (pāj), *quiz* (kwiz), *rhymes* (rīmz), *riddle* (ridəl), *rock* (rok), *scoreboard* (skōrbōrd), *shoes* (shüz), *sign* (sīn), *socks* (soks), *the* (thə), *thumb* (thum), *to* (tü), *two* (tü), *walk* (wôk), *want* (wônt), *what* (hwut), *whistle* (hwisəl)

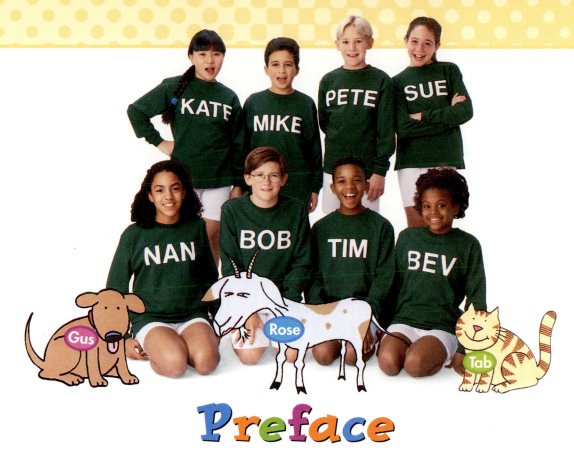

Preface

Newcomer Phonics is a highly visual program of phonics activities written especially for emerging readers in grades 3–8. The characters of the *Phonics Team* — *Nan, Bob, Tim, Bev, Kate, Mike, Pete,* and *Sue* and their pets, *Tab, Gus,* and *Rose* — are all named for short and long vowels. In each phonics section, they *hop* and *run* through easily decodable sentences full of fun and surprises.

Newcomer Phonics units feature carefully controlled, high-frequency words embedded in the context of simple sentences with clear illustrations. Pages are designed to reinforce conversational vocabulary for new English language learners and help them transfer decoding skills from their native language into English.

New sounds and spellings are highlighted in red at the top of each page. Words with irregular pronunciations are indicated by a special icon ⚷ that refers students to the Pronunciation Key on the facing page and at the end of the book.

Newcomer Phonics activities progress from one-syllable, short-vowel words (*Nan has a hat*) to long-vowel words (*Mike rides a bike*) to more complex sound-letter correspondence (*Math problems make you think*). Many activities also include specific elements for English language learners, such as (1) linguistic topics: pronouns, possessives, verbs, adjectives, prepositions, and question forms and (2) ELD themes: classroom, family, food, clothes, and weather words. Finally, at the end of each unit, there is a humorous story booklet featuring the antics of the *Phonics Team*, which students can remove, read to themselves, and take home for their own enjoyment.

Contents

Nan has a cat.   map   hat   bag   pan

Match the sentences with the pictures.

1. Nan has a cat.

2. Nan has a map.

3. Nan has a hat.

4. Nan has a bag.

5. Nan has a pan.

a

b

c

d

e

Tab

man   mat   van   Nan taps a bag.   Tab, the fat cat

Write the word that finishes each sentence.

1 Nan has a _____mat_____ .

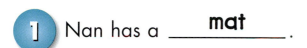

2 Nan has a _____ .

3 Nan taps a _____ .

4 The man has a _____ .

5 Nan has a _____ .

Bob can jog.   Bob hops.   dog   doll   on the rock   off the rock

Match the sentences with the pictures.

1 Bob can jog.

2 Bob hops on the rock.

3 The cat hops off the rock.

4 The dog has a mat.

5 The doll has a hat.

a

b

c

d

e

Can/Cannot

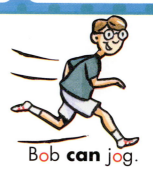

Bob **can** jog.   The doll **cannot** jog.   pot

Write the word to match the picture.

1 The doll __**cannot**__ hop.
         can/cannot

2 Nan _____ jog.
     can/cannot

3 Bob _____ hop on a rock.
     can/cannot

4 A van _____ jog.
     can/cannot

5 A pot _____ hop.
     can/cannot

Tim sits on a hill.

Tim hits the ball.

Tim has a mitt.

Match the sentences with the pictures.

a

Tim

1 Tim can hit.

2 Tim sits on a mat.

3 Tab sits on the mitt.

4 Tim has a mitt.

5 A cat sits on a hill.

b

c

d

e

 is sad/is not sad  is hot/is not hot

is big/is not big (little)   is mad/is not mad

Write the word or words to match the picture.

1 Tim _____**is**_____ mad.
      is/is not

2 The pan _____ hot.
        is/is not

3 The van _____ big.
        is/is not

4 Nan _____ sad.
      is/is not

5 The cat _____ big.
        is/is not

The bag **of** Tim = Tim's bag

Match the sentences that mean the same thing.

1 The hat **of Tim** is not big.

2 The cat **of Nan** is on the mat.

3 The bag **of Tim** is big.

4 The dog **of Bob** can jog.

a **Tim's** bag is big.

b **Nan's** cat is on the mat.

c **Bob's** dog can jog.

d **Tim's** hat is not big.

On/Off

Write the word to match the picture.

1 Nan's hat is ____**on**____ the dog.

on/off

2 Tab is _____ the mat.

on/off

3 Bob is _____ the rock.

on/off

Tab is mad.

8

The Big Bag

1

The bag hops on the mat.
Hop. Hop.
Is Tab in the bag?

6

3

Nan has a big bag.
The bag has a hat in it.
The bag has a map in it.

Nan taps the bag.
The bag hops.
A bag cannot hop!

Review: a, o, i | Final X

 fox
 box
6 six
 ax
socks

Circle *yes* if the sentence matches the picture.
Circle *no* if it does not.

1 Bob has socks.   yes   (no)

2 The mitt is in the box.   yes   no

3 Tab is a fox.   yes   no

4 Tim has an ax.   yes   no

5 Nan has six hats.   yes   no

Gus can run. bus up bug Nan hugs Gus.

Match the sentences with the pictures.

1 Gus can run.

2 The bus is big.

3 Bob hugs Gus.

4 The jack-in-the-box pops up.

5 The bug is not big.

a

b

c

d

e

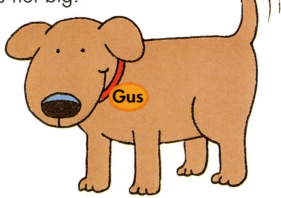

u | **Gus has fun.**

Gus has fun.   tub   nut   rug   sun

Write the word that finishes each sentence.

1 Gus has fun in the ____tub____ .

2 Gus sits on the _____ .

3 Gus runs in the _____ .

4 Gus has a _____ .

5 Bob has a _____ .

Bev has a pen. bed red get on the bus get off the bus

Match the sentences with the pictures.

1 Bev has a pen.

2 Bev gets off the bus.

3 Tab gets on the bed.

4 Bev's bed is red.

5 The pen is not red.

a

b

c

d

e

bell   pets   men   seven   leg

Circle *yes* or *no* to answer the questions.

1 Is Bev's leg up?   yes   no

2 Is Bev in a van?   yes   no

3 Can Bev's doll run?   yes   no

4 Can the pets run?   yes   no

5 Can seven men jog?   yes   no

A Pen

Lots of Pens

Write the word or words to match the picture.

a pen, ~~pens~~

a cat, cats

a bell, bells

a hat, hats

~~a bed~~, beds

a dog, dogs

a leg, legs

a bug, bugs

a bag, bags

a nut, nuts

1 pens

2 a bed

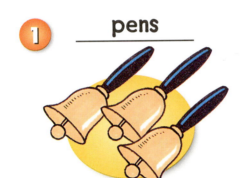

3 _____

4 _____

5 _____

6 _____

7 _____

8 _____

Gus is sad.

The Bus

8

1

✂- -

Gus hops on the bus.

Get off the bus, Gus!
Gus! Get off the bus!

6

3

Bob is on the bus.
Nan is on the bus.
Tim is on the bus.

2

7

Gus is not on the bus.
Gus is a dog.
A dog cannot get on the bus.

4

5

Review: Nan, Tab, Bob, Tim, Gus, and Bev

Look at the picture. Choose a word from the box to finish each sentence.

___**X**___ up   _____ Gus   _____ rock

_____ sits   _____ red   _____ Nan

---

1 The sun is ____**up**____ .

2 Bob, Bev, and _____ jog.

3 _____ has a bag.

4 Nan's bag is _____ .

5 Tab hops on a _____ .

6 Tim _____ on a mat.

| ten o'clock | flag | plant | black pot | glass | sled |

Match the sentences with the pictures.

1 Nan has a flag.

2 It is ten o'clock.

3 The glass is not red.

4 The plant is in the sun.

5 The sled is not black.

a

b

c

d

e

Circle *yes* if the sentence matches the picture.
Circle *no* if it does not.

1. Gus is in the class.   yes   no

2. A bus is in the class.   yes   no

3. Gus has Nan's bag.   yes   no

4. The bag is black.   yes   no

5. Gus is on a sled.   yes   no

6. A bell is in the class.   yes   no

7. Gus has a glass.   yes   no

8. Gus is a black dog.   yes   no

9. A flag is in the class.   yes   no

10. It is ten o'clock.   yes   no

On the **Grass**

grass   frog   brick   truck   crab   dress

Match the sentences with the pictures.

a

1. The frog is on the grass.

b

2. The crab is not on the grass.

c

3. Bev has a red dress.

d

4. Bob drops a red brick.

e

5. Gus is in the truck.

On the Steps

steps   spill   snack   swim   Bev skips.   smell

Match the sentences with the pictures.

1. A big stick is on the steps.

2. Bev skips.

3. The snack spills.

4. Nan can smell the snack.

5. Tim can swim.

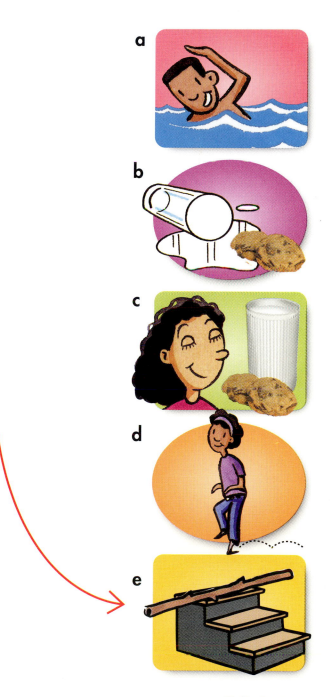

a

b

c

d

e

Initial Blends: *st, sp, sn, sw, sk, sm*; Verbs: *spill, swim, skip, smell*

On the Sand

sand   milk   jump   tank   gift

Write the word that finishes each sentence.

1 Gus runs on the __**sand**__.

2 Bob can _____ on a rock.

3 Bev has a glass of _____.

4 A frog is in the _____.

5 Tim has a _____.

Next to Bev 🔑

nest — desk — Help! — belt — tent

Bob is next to Bev.

Write the word that finishes each sentence.

1. The frog is ___next___ to the rock.

2. The belt is on Nan's _____.

3. Gus is next to the _____.

4. The frog is in a _____.

5. Tim yells, "_____!"

Quack Quiz 🔑

**Circle *yes* if the sentence matches the picture.
Circle *no* if it does not.**

1. Gus and Bev swim in the pond.   yes   (no)
2. A frog is not on the rock; it is gone.   yes   no
3. Tab is on a desk.   yes   no
4. Ducks swim in the pond.   yes   no
5. A flag is on the rock.   yes   no
6. Nan's belt is on the sand.   yes   no
7. Ducks can quack.   yes   no
8. Tab can quack.   yes   no
9. A crab is in the pond.   yes   no
10. The pond has grass in it.   yes   no

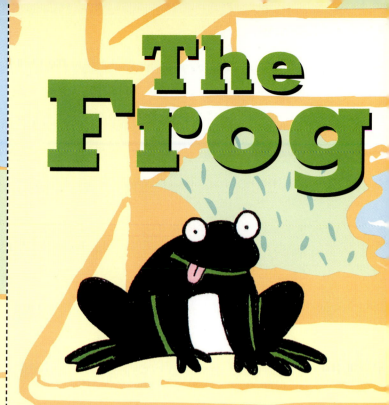

The Frog

"Help! Get the frog!" yells Nan.

"It is on the steps!"

But the frog is gone…

It hops on the big map.

It hops off the big map.

It lands on Nan's snack and spills the milk.

Next, the frog jumps on Bob's bag…

and hops on Tim's leg…

and jumps on Bev's desk.

A glass tank is in the class.

The tank has a plant, sand, and grass in it.

A little pond is in the tank.

A black frog swims in the pond.

But the frog is not in the glass tank.

It is not on the desk.

It is not on the clock.

The flag hops and jumps.

The frog pops up.

Review: Blends and Short Vowels

~~cat~~	grass	bus	pens	hit
desk	dog	jump	dress	sits

Self Test: Write the word that finishes each sentence.

1 Tab is a fat _____**cat**_____ .

2 Gus is a big _____ .

3 Tim can _____ the ball.

4 Gus and Bob can _____ .

5 Nan and Bob get on the _____ .

6 Bev has ten red _____ .

7 A frog is in the _____ .

8 A plant is on the _____ .

9 Tim _____ on a hill.

10 Bev has a red _____ .

Kate takes a plate.

waves in a lake

Kate makes a cake.

Kate wakes up.

snake

Match the sentences with the pictures.

Kate

a

1 Kate makes a sand cake.

2 Kate wakes up at six o'clock.

b

3 Kate's plate has grapes on it.

c

4 The lake has waves.

d

e

5 The snake is not in the lake.

Bob and Nan say, "Hey, Kate!"

Hey, Kate!

Kate plays on a gray day.

Kate lays a crayon on the desk.

Write the word to match the picture.

1 Kate and Tab ____**play**____ .
    say/play

2 The crayon is _____ .
    gray/red

3 Kate lays a _____ of grapes on the desk.
    plate/snake

4 Bob and Nan _____ , "Hey!"
    play/say

Hey!

5 Kate _____ up at ten o'clock.
    waves/wakes

ai Kate waits.

It is **not** a **grea**t day.

Kate w**ai**ts in the r**ai**n and h**ai**l.

a sn**ai**l in a p**ai**l

tr**ai**n

Match the sentences with the pictures.

a

1 Kate waits at a bus stop in the rain.

b

2 Kate takes the red pail away.

c

3 Kate gets on the train at eight o'clock.

d

4 "The day is great!" says Kate.

e

5 Hail lands on the snail.

ace age — Kate's Face on the Page

Kate's face is happy.   Kate and Nan race.   page   cage   stage

Circle *yes* if the sentence matches the pictures above.
Circle *no* if it does not.

1. Kate has a sad face.   yes   (no)

2. The page has a cage on it.   yes   no

3. Kate and the dog race on the grass.   yes   no

The page has…/Lots of pages have…

Write the word that finishes each sentence.

1. The cage **has** a ___snake___ in it.

2. Tim and Bob **have** red _____ .

3. Kate and Nan **have** black _____ .

It's the same.

it is	=	it's
is not	=	isn't
cannot	=	can't
let us	=	let's

Match the sentences that mean the same.

1 **It is** a great day.

2 A snake **cannot** make a cake.

3 **Let us** take a snack.

4 The snail **is not** in the pail.

a The snail **isn't** in the pail.

b **It's** a great day.

c **Let's** take a snack.

d A snake **can't** make a cake.

Two words can mean almost the same.

Read the first sentence. Finish the second sentence with the word that means almost the same.

1 A frog can **hop**. = A frog can ___**jump**___ .
$\qquad$ jump/walk

2 Bob can **jog**. = Bob can _____ .
$\qquad$ swim/run

3 Kate has a **picnic**. = Kate has a _____ .
$\qquad$ snack/snake

Gus races in the lake,
...and the snake gets away.

8

The Lake

1

But wait!

It's not a stick.

It's a gray snake.

"Hey, Gus!" yells Kate.

"Drop the snake!"

But Gus runs and runs.

6

3

Kate and Nan wake up at eight.

The rain is gone, and the day is great.

"Let's have a picnic at the lake," says Kate.

"Great!" says Nan. "Let's take Gus."

Kate and Nan make a snack.

2

7

Kate takes grapes and cake.

Gus helps. Gus takes the plates.

At the lake, Nan lays the picnic on the sand.

Kate jumps in the waves.

Gus takes a stick and plays.

4

5

Review: Kate's Great Day

Circle *yes* if the sentence matches the picture.
Circle *no* if it does not.

1. Kate and Nan play on the sand.   (yes)   no

2. Rain lands on the cake.   yes   no

3. A duck swims in the waves.   yes   no

4. Hail makes the day gray.   yes   no

5. The pail has crayons in it.   yes   no

6. Eight snails play on a stick.   yes   no

7. A train is on the page.   yes   no

8. The lake is gray.   yes   no

9. A gray snake waits on the rock.   yes   no

10. Kate's face is sad.   yes   no

Mike rides a bike. | Mike likes pie. | **5** five | **9** nine | kite

Match the sentences with the pictures.

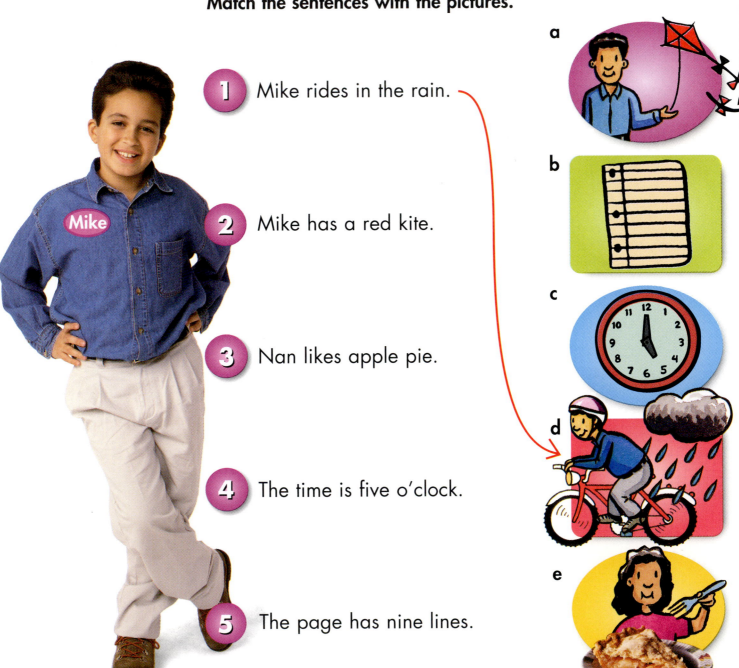

Mike

1 Mike rides in the rain.

2 Mike has a red kite.

3 Nan likes apple pie.

4 The time is five o'clock.

5 The page has nine lines.

a

b

c

d

e

I –y I like my bike.

"Hi! My bike is by the slide."

eyes / smile   A kite can fly in the sky.   cry / cries

Write the word that finishes each sentence.

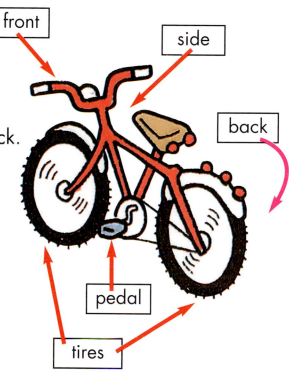

front   side

back

pedal

tires

1 Mike's bike is by the _____**slide**_____ .

2 A _____ has tires in front and back.

3 Mike says, "Hi! _____ am Mike."

4 A bike is not like a kite.

A kite can _____ in the sky.

5 Mike's face is not sad.

It has a big _____ .

Yikes!

STOP

6 Mike stops and _____ , "Yikes!"

igh Lights at Night

bright lights at night

Wind makes the kite glide high.

left/right

Write the word that finishes each sentence.

1. Mike has bright ____lights____ on his bike.

2. Mike can ride the bike at _____.

3. A big _____ is on the front of Mike's bike.

4. The light of the sun is _____.

5. Mike's kite can glide _____ in the sky.

6. The kite is in Mike's _____ hand.

ire **ice** Fire and Ice

ice

a wide sign

Mice bite.

fire

a flat tire

Mice hide.

Circle *yes* if the sentence is true.
Circle *no* if the sentence is not true.

1 A fire is hot. (yes) no

2 Mice can fly in the sky. yes no

3 A stop sign is red. yes no

4 Ice is hot. yes no

5 A dog can bite a ball. yes no

6 A kite can bite a light. yes no

7 Bikes have nine tires. yes no

8 A frog can hide in the grass. yes no

9 A pen is wide and big. yes no

10 A flat tire can make a bike stop. yes no

Rhymes

Rhymes have the same end sounds.
Example: *Mike* and *like* rhyme.

~~lake~~	face	man	night
sky	tire	hot	run	train
yell	day	page	wide
sand	snail	class	nine	jog

Find the word from the box above that rhymes.
Write it on the line.

1. take ___lake___

2. hand _____

3. ride _____

4. race _____

5. van _____

6. light _____

7. fly _____

8. fire _____

9. line _____

10. dog _____

11. not _____

12. cage _____

13. sun _____

14. rain _____

15. bell _____

16. play _____

17. grass _____

18. pail _____

"Yikes!" cries Mike.

"My bike has a flat tire!"

Mike is mad.

Gus hides in the grass.

8

The Bike

1

Mike rides by Bob and Gus.

Gus jogs by the side of Mike's bike.

"Gus likes the bike!" cries Mike.

But the bike tire hits a rock.

Mike jumps off the bike.

6

3

Mike sits high on his bike.

It's a bright, red bike.

Mike can ride fast and race on it.

It has wide, black tires and blue pedals.

On the back, it has five little lights.

Mike can ride his bike day and night.

2

7

The bike can race up hills and slide on sand.

It can glide like a kite.

"My bike can fly!" cries Mike.

"I can ride like the wind. I can race day and night. I can ride miles and miles!"

4

5

Review: My Life

Write about yourself.

1 My name is _____ .
name

2 My age is _____ .
8/9/10/11/12/13/14/other

3 I have _____ .
a pet/no pet

4 I like _____ .
cake/pie/grapes/hot dogs/other

5 I can __**X**__ ride a bike.   _____ swim.

_____ jump high.   _____ make a cake.

_____ fly a kite.   _____ run fast.

_____ hit a baseball.   _____ .

A rope holds Rose's nose.

Rose is a goat.

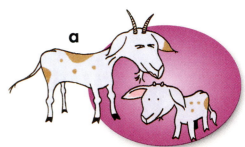

Boats float.

soap

Match the sentences with the pictures.

1 Rose walks in the road.

a

2 Rose is by the boat.

b

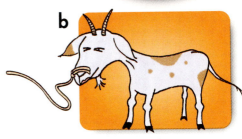

3 Rose has a little goat.

c

4 The soap floats.

d

5 A rope is on Rose's nose.

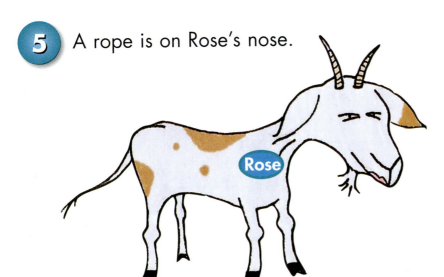

Rose

e

Plants gr**ow**.

cold sn**ow**

fast boat/sl**ow** boat

Winds bl**ow**.

wind**ow**

Write the word that finishes each sentence.

1 A rowboat is a ___**slow**___ boat.

2 Rose walks in the _____ and gets cold.

3 Cold winds _____ on the lake.

4 The desk is by the _____ .

5 Plants _____ in the sun.

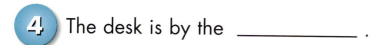

or More Sports

door

scoreboard

HOME VISITORS

four forks

Tim plays more sports.

floor

yellow corn

Circle *yes* if the sentence is true.
Circle *no* if it is not.

1 Basketball is a sport.   (yes)   no

2 Tennis is a sport.   yes   no

3 Goats can play basketball.   yes   no

4 A class has a door.   yes   no

5 A scoreboard has a score on it.   yes   no

6 Forks can run.   yes   no

7 Goats can eat yellow corn.   yes   no

8 A rowboat can fly.   yes   no

9 A train has doors.   yes   no

10 Grass grows on a floor.   yes   no

High and *low* are opposites.

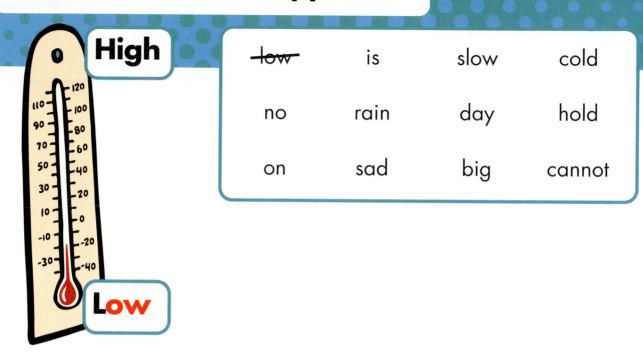

High

~~low~~	is	slow	cold
no	rain	day	hold
on	sad	big	cannot

Low

Find the word in the box that is opposite to the one below.
Write it on the line.

1. high ___low___

2. little _____

3. yes _____

4. hot _____

5. can _____

6. is not _____

7. off _____

8. fast _____

9. sun _____

10. drop _____

11. night _____

12. glad _____

e–e ea ee   Pete reads by the tree.

He sleeps by a tree.

Pete reads.

The team eats meat.

green leaf

feet

Match the sentences with the pictures.

1 Pete reads a lot.

2 He is on the green team.

3 The tree has yellow leaves.

4 Gus eats Pete's meat.

5 Pete sleeps till nine o'clock.

a

b

c

PETE

d

e

The Baseball Field

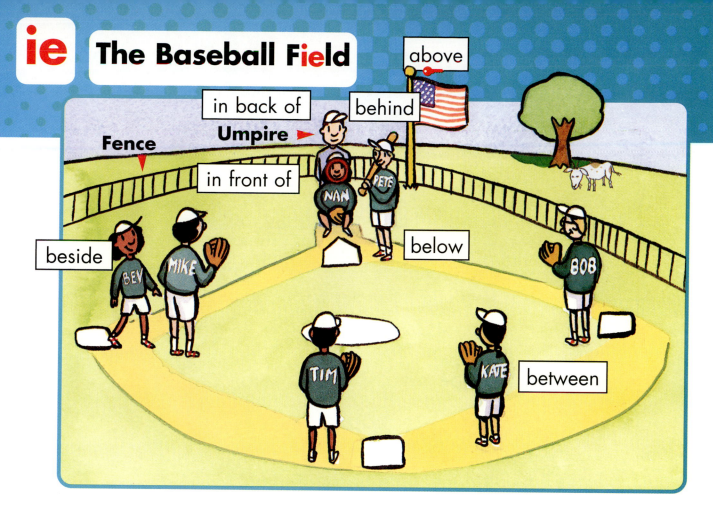

Circle _yes_ if the sentence matches the picture.
Circle _no_ if it does not.

1. Bev is beside Mike.   (yes)   no

2. The flag is above the field.   yes   no

3. Nan is in front of Pete.   yes   no

4. The fence is behind the umpire.   yes   no

5. The umpire is in back of a tree.   yes   no

6. Rose the goat is above the flag.   yes   no

7. Kate is between Bob and Tim.   yes   no

8. Pete is beside home plate.   yes   no

 **Is he a monkey?** **y** **Is he a baby?**

He likes me.

| monk**ey** | don**key** | happ**y** baby | pupp**y** | twen**ty** |

20

Write the word or words from above that answer the riddle.

1 He smiles a lot. He likes milk.

He plays on a mat. He is a ___**happy baby**___.

2 He is big and gray. He has four legs.

He likes grass. He is a _____.

3 He has four little legs. He can play ball.

He likes bones. He is a _____.

bone

4 It is the same as six and six and eight.

It is _____.

bananas

5 He plays in trees. He can jump high. He has feet and

hands. He likes bananas. He is a _____.

eer ear The d**ee**r is n**ear**.

Pete's **ear**s can h**ear**.

He is fourteen y**ear**s old.

The d**ee**r is n**ear**.

A nice cl**ear** sky

Write the word that finishes each sentence.

1 The ___deer___ sees a fox.

2 The fox has big _____ .

It can hear the deer.

3 The sun is bright and the sky is _____ .

4 Nan is ten _____ old.

5 The puppy sits _____ Pete.

ue u-e Sue plays the flute.

Sue plays a tune on the flute.

music

Sue uses a blue pen and glue.

a huge cube

Match the sentences with the pictures.

a

1 Sue plays the flute.

b

2 Sue has huge blue eyes.

c

3 Sue has a blue bike.

d

4 Sue uses the glue.

e

5 The glass has ice cubes in it.

Sue

ou | **Do y*ou*...?**

Do y*ou* like s*ou*p?

Yes, I do.

No, I do not (don't).

j*ui*ce

Two gr*ou*ps of fr*ui*t

2

Circle *yes* if you do. Circle *no* if you do not.

(1) Do you like fruit? — ⭕ Yes, I do.   No, I don't.

(2) Do you like grape juice? — Yes, I do.   No, I don't.

(3) Do you like to play baseball? — Yes, I do.   No, I don't.

(4) Do you walk to class? — Yes, I do.   No, I don't.

(5) Do you have a dog? — Yes, I do.   No, I don't.

(6) Do you have a blue pen? — Yes, I do.   No, I don't.

(7) Do you have a cat? — Yes, I do.   No, I don't.

(8) Do you help in class? — Yes, I do.   No, I don't.

(9) Do you play basketball? — Yes, I do.   No, I don't.

(10) Do you sit in the front of the class? — Yes, I do.   No, I don't.

 **ew** **Old/New** **Many/Few**

 old hat

 new hat

 many cubes

 a few cubes

~~few~~	sunny	happy	low	behind	sleep	day
ride	feet	hold	get on	wait	huge	above

**Find the word from the box above that is opposite.
Write it on the line.**

1. many **few**

2. sad _____

3. high _____

4. rainy _____

5. below _____

6. drop _____

7. head _____

8. in front _____

9. night _____

10. little _____

11. go _____

12. wake up _____

13. walk _____

14. get off _____

The ball lands behind the fence right beside Rose.

The umpire yells, "Home run!"

"Don't let Rose get the ball!" cries Mike.

But no ball is in the grass.

Rose likes home runs.

8

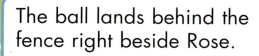

Go, Pete!

1

A low, slow ball floats near his feet.

Pete lets it go. He taps his bat and waits.

The next ball is a fast ball.

He steps up. He hits it.

The ball goes back... back... back to the trees.

It's a huge hit! The green team cries, "Go, Pete!"

6

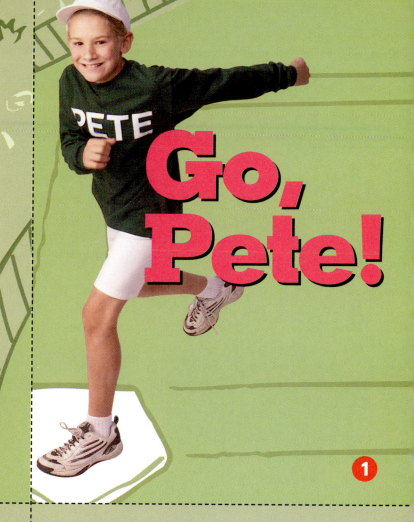

3

Pete is on the green team.

He steps up to the plate and taps his bat.

It's a new bat, and he can't wait to use it.

The blue team is in the field.

Pete sees Kate and Mike.

He hears Sue say, "Go, Pete!"

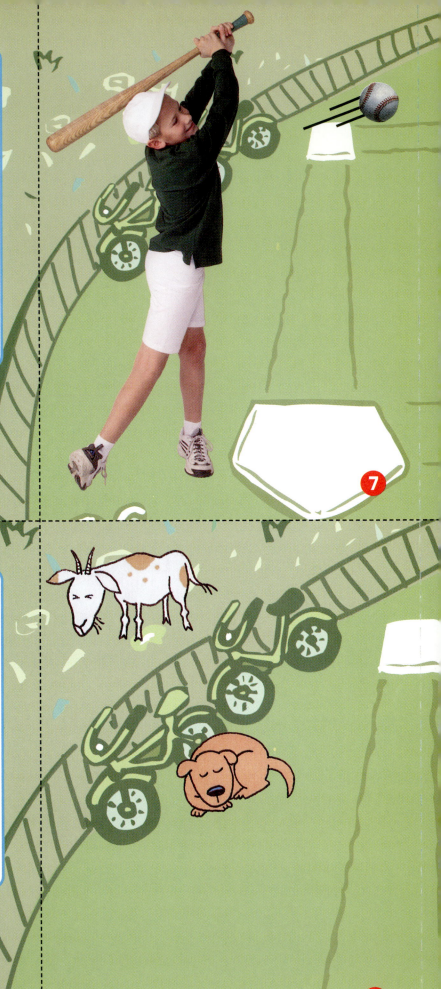

The day is sunny and clear.

Gus sleeps by the bikes.

Rose eats grass behind the fence.

A little wind blows the trees.

It's a nice day for a baseball game.

Pete waits. He taps his bat on the plate.

Review: Long Vowels

float	blue	sport	low	go	hold	grow
monkey	hear	sleep	tree	music	donkey	blow

Use eight of the words from the box above to finish the sentences.

1 A rowboat can _____float_____ in a lake.

2 The wind can _____ in an open window.

3 A plant can _____ in the sun by a window.

4 Basketball is a _____ like baseball and tennis.

5 A _____ has green leaves.

6 A _____ is gray, has four legs and big ears, and eats grass.

7 A flute can make _____ .

8 The sky is clear and _____ on a nice day.

sh | **Ship or Sheep?**

sheep on a ship   shoes   She washes dishes.   fish   brush

Match the sentences with the pictures.

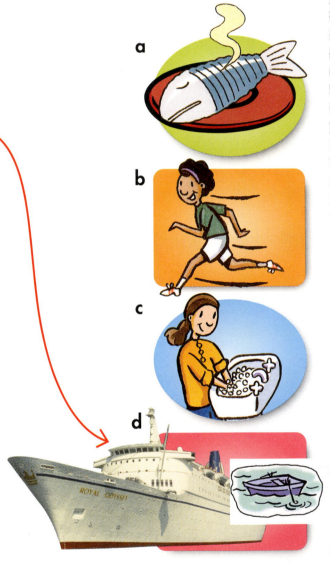

a

b

c

d

ROYAL ODYSSEY

e

1 A big ship is beside the blue boat.

2 Four sheep eat grass.

3 She runs fast in new tennis shoes.

4 Wash your hands before you eat.

5 The dish has a fish on it.

ph On the Phone

 telephone  earphones 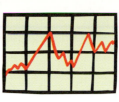 elephant graph  Phonics Team photo

Fill in the phone conversation. Write the words that finish each sentence.

Pete: Hi, Mike.

Mike: Hi, Pete.

Pete: Do you want to _____**play baseball**_____ ?
play baseball / ride an elephant

Mike: Sure, do you have your _____ ?
new earphones / new bat

Pete: Yes. Do you _____ ?
have a mitt / have a dish

Mike: Yes. Can Kate play _____ ?
on the ship / on the team

Pete: Sure, _____ .
he can play / she can play

Mike: Okay, let's play on _____ .
the big field / the big sheep

Pete: Okay. Bye, Mike.

Mike: Bye!

thick/thin   thumb   throw   bath   Kate thinks.   three months

Circle *yes* if the sentence is true. Circle *no* if the sentence is not true. Write or copy the true sentence.

1 A leaf is thick and black.   yes   ⃝no⃝

A leaf is thin and green.
_____

2 Feet have five thumbs.   yes   no
_____

3 Math problems make you think.   yes   no
_____

4 You can take a bath in a bathtub.   yes   no
_____

5 A frog can throw a baseball.   yes   no
_____

6 A year has three months.   yes   no
_____

Bob and Gus dash.

thump

Kate shakes the mat.

splash

Write the word that finishes each sentence.

1 Tim plays ball with ____Mike____ and lands with a thump.

2 Nan is in the rowboat with _____ and hears a splash.

3 Gus dashes on the sand with _____.

4 Sue sits with _____ and plays the flute.

5 Tab is in the grass with _____.

6 Kate shakes a mat near Pete and _____.

th This _____ rhymes with **that** _____.

Sheep sleep.

Read the word on this side. Then write the rhyme from that side.

1 dish _____fish_____

2 dash _____

3 that _____

4 phone _____

5 shake _____

6 thump _____

7 coat _____

8 throw _____

9 bath _____

10 sheep _____

11 shine _____

12 three _____

grow

jump

math

tree

~~fish~~

hat

line

make

crash

bone

boat

sleep

Bob is on the phone and can't stop Gus.

Gus dashes by like a wet fish.

The back door is open, and he races onto the grass.

Bob hears: Thump!

SHAKE, SHAKE, SHAKE! Thump!

8

The Bath

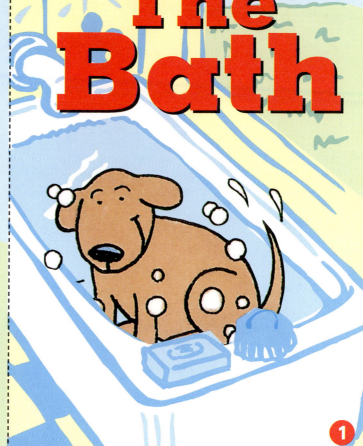

1

Then Bob hears the phone.

"Oh, no!" he says. "Sit, Gus. Stay!"

But Gus jumps onto the floor with a splash.

He slips on the wet floor.

SHAKE, SHAKE, SHAKE!

The brushes crash.

Gus dashes for the door.

6

3

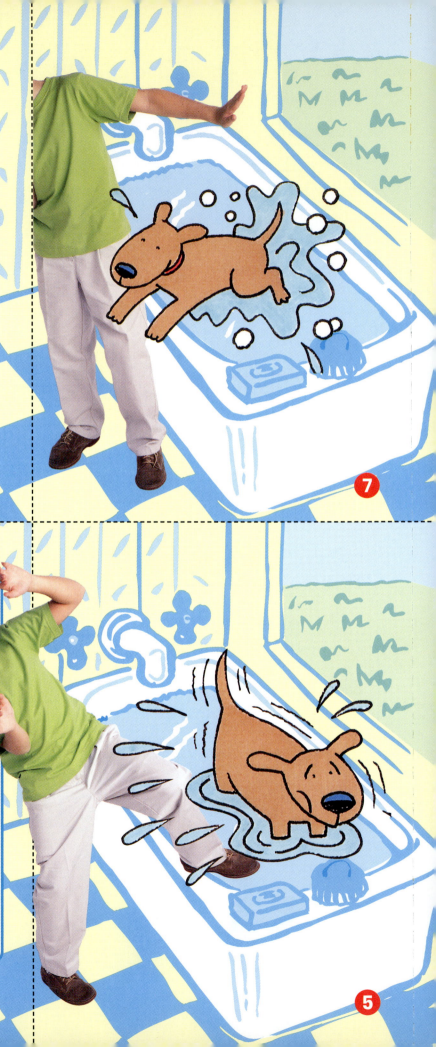

Splash! Splash!

SHAKE! SHAKE! SHAKE!

Gus is in the bathtub.

He splashes and shakes three more times.

Bob takes the soap and washes his back.

Then he washes all the soap off.

He holds on to Gus with his hand.

Gus is not happy.

His thick coat is wet and cold.

He wants to jump from the bathtub.

But Bob holds him back and washes his ears.

Gus goes SHAKE, SHAKE, SHAKE.

Bob gets wet, and the floor gets wet.

Review: These Clothes, Those Clothes

These shoes are blue.

Those shoes are red.

Which of **these** clothes go with **those** clothes?
Match the clothes that are the same colors and write the answers.

those green shoes   those blue shoes
that black hat   ~~those tan socks~~
those red shoes   that red and blue cap
that yellow rain hat

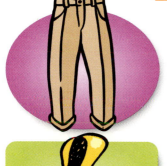

1 these tan pants   **those tan socks**

2 these blue socks _____

3 this yellow raincoat _____

4 this green dress _____

5 this red and blue jacket _____

6 this black coat _____

7 these red shorts _____

Review of Digraphs: /sh/ sh, /th/ th; Demonstrative Pronouns and Adjectives: these, those

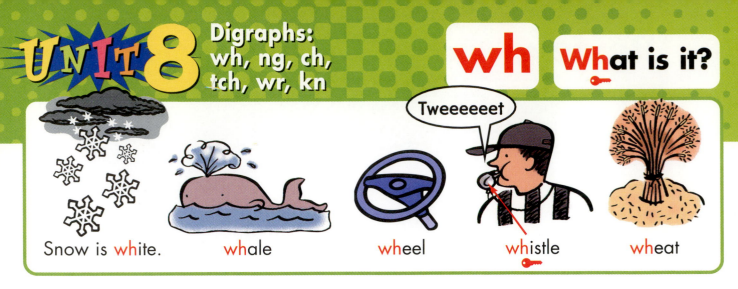

UNIT 8

**Digraphs:
wh, ng, ch,
tch, wr, kn**

wh **Wh**at is it?

Snow is white.   whale   wheel   whistle   wheat

Draw a line to the sentence that answers the question.

1 What is a whale?

2 What is a wheel?

3 What is wheat?

4 What is a whistle?

5 What is snow like?

6 What is a ship?

7 What is a bathtub?

a It is a plant.

b It is a big animal.

c It is white and cold.

d It is a huge boat.

e It is what you sit in to wash yourself.

f It is what you blow to stop a game.

g It is what makes a truck go left.

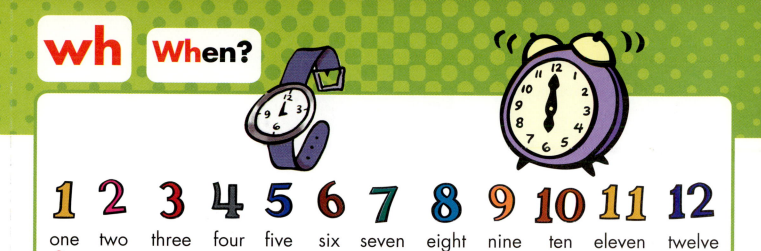

wh | **Wh**en?

1	2	3	4	5	6	7	8	9	10	11	12
one	two	three	four	five	six	seven	eight	nine	ten	eleven	twelve

Write the word from the box above that answers each question.

1 When do you wake up?   I wake up at ____**seven**____ .

2 When do you go to class?   I go to class at _____ .

3 When do you go back home?   I go home at _____ .

4 When do you have a snack?   I have a snack at _____ .

5 When do you wash your face?   I wash my face at _____ .

6 When do you go bed?   I go to bed at _____ .

Unit 8

ng Sing a song.

Sue sings a song.   The king has a ring.   a long string   swing

Write the word that finishes each sentence.

1. Sue sings a ___**song**___ .
   string/song

2. The kite has a long _____ .
   string/swing

3. The _____ hangs from the tree.
   song/swing

4. The _____ has a big ring.
   king/string

5. Nan can make the _____ go high.
   swing/ring

6. A snake is _____ , like a stick.
   song/long

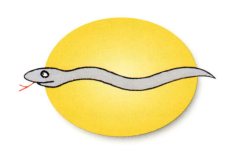

Digraphs: /ng/ng; Verb: sing

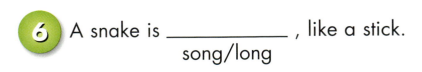

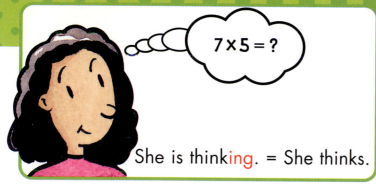

-ing Nan is thinking.

$7 \times 5 = ?$

She is thinking. = She thinks.

Write the letter of the picture that matches the sentence on the line.

a

b

1. Sue is singing a song. __h__

2. Pete is reading. _____

3. Bev is washing the dishes. _____

c

d

4. Tim is swimming. _____

5. Mike is riding a bike. _____

6. Pete is sleeping. _____

e

f

7. Gus is eating the meat. _____

8. The frog is jumping. _____

g

h

ch | **Cheese for Lunch**

cheese   sandwich   lunchbox   chicken   peach   chalk

Write the word that finishes each sentence.

1. Pete has cheese in his __sandwich__ .

2. The sandwich is in Pete's _____ .

3. Kate is eating a _____ .

4. The box of white _____ is on the desk.

5. Tab sees a _____ by the tree.

tch Catch that pitch!

Tim can ca**tch** a fast pi**tch**.   Bob wa**tch**es his wa**tch**.   scra**tch**   ma**tch**

Write the word that finishes each sentence.

1 Tim likes to catch, and Pete likes to _____**pitch**_____.

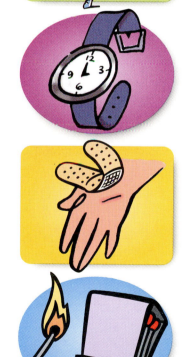

2 Bob has a _____ that says three o'clock.

3 Kate has a _____ on her hand.

4 Nan says, "Don't play with that _____!"

5 Mike likes to _____ baseball games on TV.

wr Right or Wrong?   kn Do you know?

21-9=???
I don't **know**.

It's **wr**ong.   Mike likes to **wr**ite.   **kn**ee   **kn**ife

Circle *right* if the sentence is correct. Circle *wrong* if it is not correct.

1. Students write on a desk. — (right)   wrong
2. Your knee is near your face. — right   wrong
3. Cats can write. — right   wrong
4. Math problems make you think. — right   wrong
5. 21−9=11 — right   wrong
6. Dogs and cats know math. — right   wrong
7. You can drink milk with a knife. — right   wrong
8. You can make a sandwich with cheese in it. — right   wrong
9. A peach is a fruit. — right   wrong
10. Cats can make a scratch on your hand. — right   wrong
11. A watch goes on your leg. — right   wrong
12. You can catch a ball with a mitt. — right   wrong

7. When can a sheep write his name?

7. When he has a pen.

8

Ask Me a Riddle

1

5. When is a king like a phone?

5. When he has a ring.

6

2. What does a beach have for lunch?

2. A *sandwich.*

3

1. What does the lake say to the beach?

1. Nothing. It just waves.

2

6. When he catches flies.

7

3. What does a snake like to sing?

3. A longggggggggg songggggggggg.

4

4. What goes ding, dong, ding, dong, splash?

4. A bell in a well.

5

Review: Words that Rhyme

dish whale scratch wheat
wrong shine king knee know
that shake sheep shoe
write when bath

Write the rhyming word from the box on the line next to each word below.

1. fish ___dish___

2. then _____

3. cat _____

4. snake _____

5. ring _____

6. long _____

7. line _____

8. math _____

9. meat _____

10. white _____

11. blue _____

12. sleep _____

13. three _____

14. snow _____

15. snail _____

16. catch _____

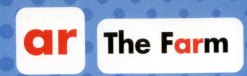 **ar** **The Farm**

farm: barn and garden

a car in a park

Stars are bright in the dark.

arm

Match the sentences with the pictures.

a

1. A barn is on the farm.

b

2. Kate's arm is inside the car.

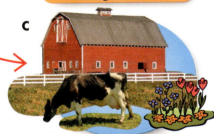
c

3. The park has a garden and a swing.

d

4. The sky is dark when it rains.

e

5. The car has a star on the front.

er Summer and Winter Weather

Bev's mother and sisters in the summer

Her father and brother in the winter

Look at the pictures above.
Write the word that finishes each sentence.

1 Bev's mother and sisters are on the beach in the _____**summer**_____ .
summer/winter

2 Her _____ has a red hat for the cold winter weather.
mother/brother

3 Bev's brother is riding on a sled in the _____ .
summer/winter

4 Her _____ is with her mother on the beach.
sister/brother

5 Bev's _____ is walking in the snow by the sled.
father/mother

ir ur Birds and Turtles

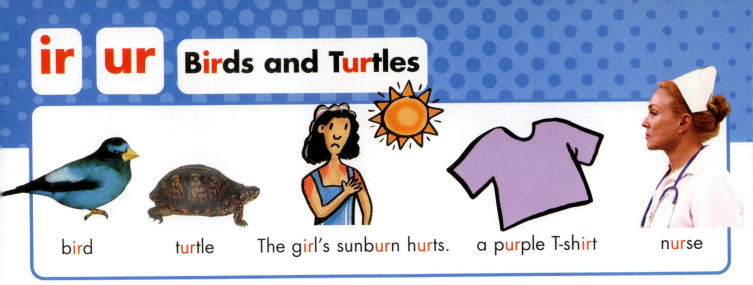

bird   turtle   The girl's sunburn hurts.   a purple T-shirt   nurse

Circle *yes* if the sentence is true. Circle *no* if the sentence is not true.

1. A turtle can fly.   yes   (no)

2. Birds can fly.   yes   no

3. Nan's sunburn hurts.   yes   no

4. The turtle is purple.   yes   no

5. Nan is a girl.   yes   no

6. Nan has a red shirt.   yes   no

7. The nurse has a purple dress.   yes   no

8. The T-shirt is purple.   yes   no

"Oh, no!" says Nan.

"My shirt and shoes are all wet.

This weather is for the birds!"

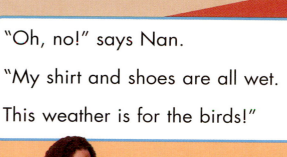

8

The Farm

1

The sky over the barn gets dark.

A summer wind blows the trees.

"Let's go!" says Nan to her sister. "It's going to rain!"

Thunder crashes, and the girls dash into the barn.

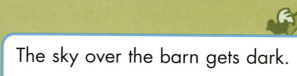

6

3

It is summer on the farm.

Nan is in the garden with her sister.

Her father is in the barn.

The sun is hot, and the girls are getting a sunburn.

"I don't like this hot weather," says Nan.

2

7

Nan's brother is not at the farm today.

He is playing baseball at the park.

Nan's mother is with him.

"Let's go inside," says Nan. "My arms are getting red."

4

5

Review: Over/Under | Before/After

over the water

under the water

ten minutes **before** three

ten minutes **after** three

Write the word to match the picture.

1 The star is shining _____**over**_____ the barn.
over/under

2 The turtle is _____ the car.
over/under

3 The purple shirt is _____ the coat.
over/under

4 It is five minutes _____ ten.
before/after

5 It is fifteen minutes _____ six.
before/after

6 It is ten minutes _____ eight.
before/after

 oo Oops!

Oops! He sh**oo**ts and misses the h**oo**p.

f**oo**d   ball**oo**ns   b**oo**ts   sch**oo**l

Match the sentences with the pictures.

1 Oops! Gus has my food.

2 Oops! The balloons are on the roof.

3 Oops! He shoots and misses.

4 Oops! The basketball hoop is too high.

5 Oops! My boots are in the school.

a

b

c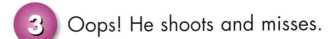

d

e

OU   Loud Sounds

Shouts are loud sounds from the mouth.

 bounce

outside

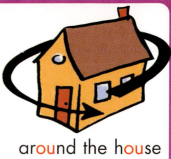 around the house

Write the word that finishes each sentence.

1 Bob shouts with his ___**mouth**___ .
   mouth / ears

2 The sound of thunder is _____ .
   loud / not loud

3 Gus is _____ the house.
   inside / outside

4 A basketball can _____ high.
   sound / bounce

5 A clock has numbers _____ it.
   under / around

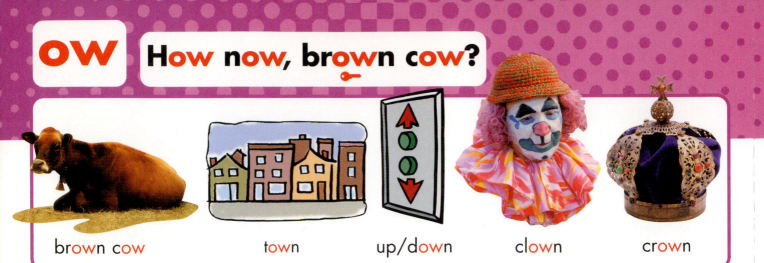

OW   How now, brown cow?

| brown cow | town | up/down | clown | crown |

Write the word that finishes each sentence.
Then read each sentence.

1 Cows can be black, white, or _____**brown**_____ .
clown / brown

2 A king has a _____ .
crown / cow

3 Bev lives on a farm, not in a _____ .
town / down

4 The face of the _____ has a big smile.
clown / crown

5 Rains falls _____ from the clouds.
up / down

oy oi Toys can make noise.

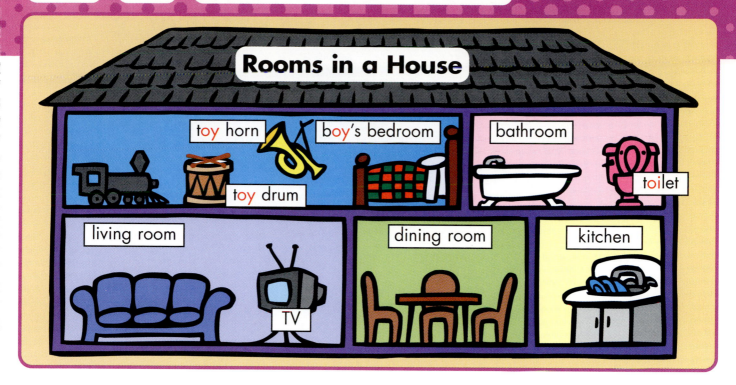

Rooms in a House

toy horn · boy's bedroom · bathroom · toilet · toy drum · living room · TV · dining room · kitchen

Circle *yes* if the sentence is true. Circle *no* if the sentence is not true.

1. The sound of a toy train comes from the boy's bedroom. (yes) no

2. The noise of dishes comes from the kitchen. yes no

3. The noise of voices on TV comes from the bathroom. yes no

4. The sound of water comes from the living room. yes no

5. The beat of a toy drum comes from the dining room. yes no

6. The toot of a toy horn comes from the boy's bedroom. yes no

7. The boy's bed is in the kitchen. yes no

8. The toilet is in the bathroom. yes no

Review: How do animals sound?

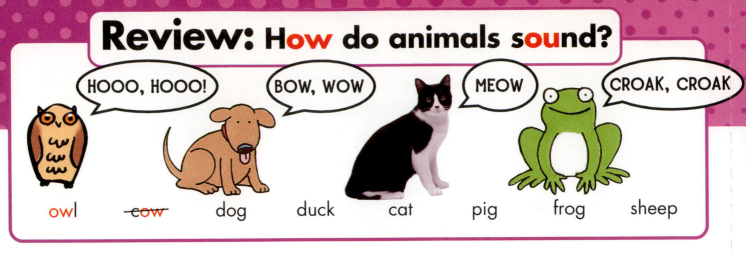

HOOO, HOOO!   BOW, WOW   MEOW   CROAK, CROAK

owl   ~~cow~~   dog   duck   cat   pig   frog   sheep

Write the animal name from the box above that answers each riddle.

1 I say MOOOO. I am big and brown. I give milk.   I am a __**cow**__ .

2 I say BOW WOW. I can live in a house or outside.   I am a _____ .

3 I say QUACK, QUACK. I swim in ponds. I can fly.   I am a _____ .

4 I say MEOW, MEOW. I eat birds. I eat mice.   I am a _____ .

5 I say OINK, OINK. I live on a farm. I eat corn.   I am a _____ .

6 I say HOOO, HOOO. I fly at night. I have big eyes.   I am an _____ .

7 I say BAAA, BAAA. I live on a farm. I eat grass.   I am a _____ .

8 I say CROAK, CROAK. I am green. I can swim.   I am a _____ .

"Let's take a team photo!" shouts a man. Nan, Bob, Tim, and Bev run to get Gus and Tab.

Kate, Mike, Pete, and Sue run to get Rose.

Drums beat. Horns toot.

What a day for the Phonics Team!

8

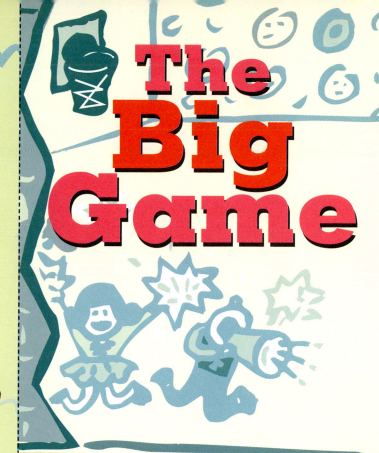

The Big Game

1

The green team wins!

Bev and Bob run outside to hug Gus.

The dog is waiting by a big table on the grass.

It has food and balloons on it.

Sue has a crown to put around Rose's ears.

Mike has clown hats for Gus and Tab.

6

3

It's the last basketball game of the school year.

Boys and girls are jumping and shouting.

"Go for the hoop! Go for the hoop!"

Drums beat. Horns toot.

"T!...E!...A!...M!
 T!...E!...A!...M!"

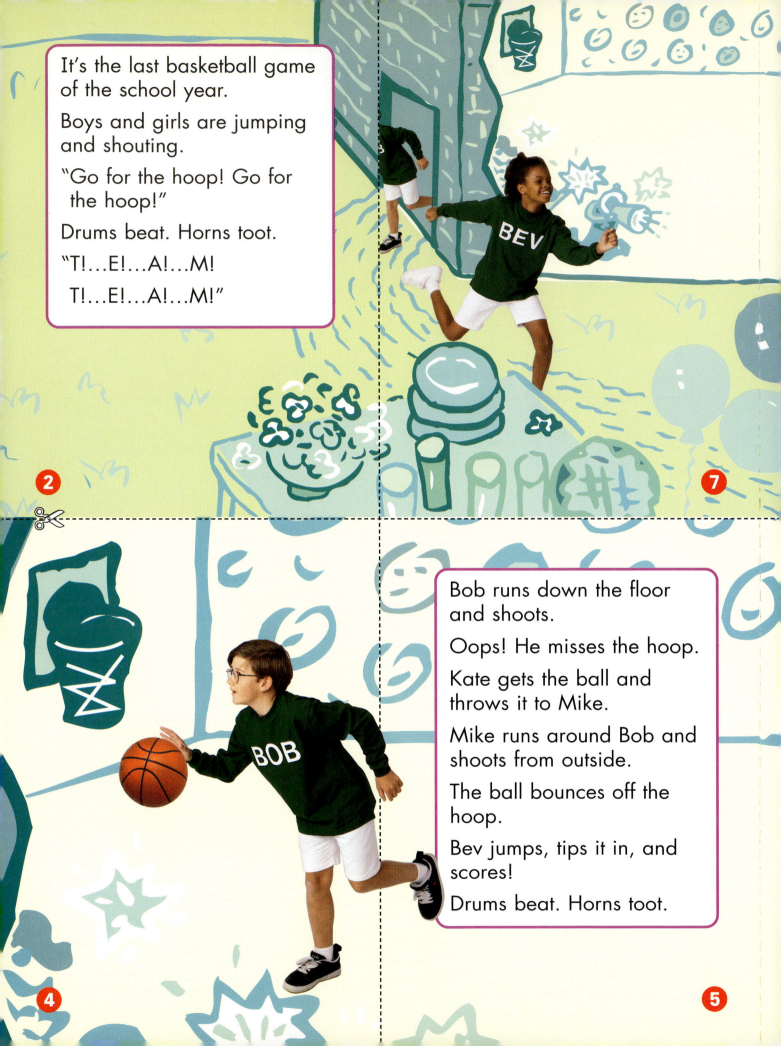

2

7

4

Bob runs down the floor and shoots.

Oops! He misses the hoop.

Kate gets the ball and throws it to Mike.

Mike runs around Bob and shoots from outside.

The ball bounces off the hoop.

Bev jumps, tips it in, and scores!

Drums beat. Horns toot.

5

Word List

a	bike	cold	fence	groups	it
above	birds	come/s	few	grow	it's
after	bite	corn	field	Gus	jack-in-the-box
age	black	cow	fifteen	gym	jog
all	blow	crab	fill	hail	juice
am	blue	crash/es	fire	hand	jump/s
an	boat	crayon	fish	hang/s	just
and	Bob	crown	five	happy	Kate
animals	bones	cry/cries	flag	has	king
apple	boots	cube	flat	hat	kitchen
are	bounce/s	dark	float/s	have	kite
arm	box	dash/es	floor	he	knee
around	boy	day	flute	head	knife
ask	brick	deer	fly	hear/s	know
at	bright	desk	food	help/s	lake
away	brother	dining room	for	her	lamp
ax	brown	dishes	forks	hey	land/s
baby	brush	do	four	hi	last
back	bug	dog	fourteen	hide	lay/s
bag	bus	doll	fox	high	leaf
ball	but	donkey	frog	hill	leaves
balloons	by	don't	from	him	left
bananas	bye	door	front	his	leg
barn	cage	down	fruit	hit/s	let
baseball	cake	dress	fun	hold/s	let's
basketball	can	drink	game	home	life
bat	cannot	drop	garden	home plate	lights
bath	can't	drum	get/s	hoop	like/s
bathroom	cap	duck	gift	hop/s	line
bathtub	car	earphones	girl	horn	little
beach	cat	ears	glad	hot	lives
beat	catch	eats	glass	hot dogs	living room
bed	chalk	eight	glide	house	long
bedroom	cheese	elephant	glue	how	lot
before	chicken	eleven	go	hug/s	loud
behind	class	eyes	goat	huge	low
bell	clear	face	gone	hurt/s	lunch
below	clock	falls	grapes	I	lunchbox
belt	closet	farm	graph	ice	mad
beside	clothes	fast	grass	in	make/s
between	clouds	fat	gray	inside	man
Bev	clown	father	great	is	many
big	coat	feet	green	isn't	**(continued on next page)**

Word List (continued)

map	on	rhyme	sleep/s	ten	under
mat	one	riddle	slide	tennis	up
match	onto	ride/s	slip	tent	us
math	oops	right	slow	test	uses
meat	open	ring	smell	that	van
men	opposites	road	smile	the	voices
mice	outside	rock	snack	then	wait/s
Mike	over	roof	snail	these	wake/s
miles	owl	rope	snake	thick	walk/s
milk	page	Rose	snow	thin	want
minutes	pail	rowboat	soap	things	wash/es
miss/es	pan	rug	socks	think	watch
mitt	pants	run/s	sofa	this	watch/es
mix	park	sad	song	those	water
monkey	peach	same	sound	three	wave/s
months	pedals	sand	soup	throw	weather
more	pen	sandwich	spill/s	thumb	well
mother	pet	say/s	splash/es	thump	wet
mouth	Pete	school	sports	thunder	whale
music	phone	score	stage	till	what
my	phonics	scoreboard	stars	Tim	wheat
name	Phonics Team	scratch	stay	time	wheel
Nan	photo	sees	steps	tip	when
near	picnic	seven	stick	tire	which
nest	pie	shake/s	stop	to	whistle
new	pig	she	string	today	white
next	pitch	sheep	students	toilet	wide
nice	plant	shelf	Sue	too	win
night	plate	shine	summer	toot	wind
nine	play/s	ship	sun	top	window
no	plop	shirt	sunburn	town	winter
noise	pond	shoes	sunny	toys	with
nose	pop/s	shorts	sunshine	train	write
not	pot	shout/s	swim/s	tree	wrong
nothing	problem	shoots	swing	truck	years
now	puppy	side	Tab	T-shirt	yell/s
numbers	purple	sign	table	tub	yellow
nurse	quack	sing/s	take/s	tune	yes
nut	quiz	sister	tan	turtles	you
o'clock	race/s	sit/s	tank	TV	your
of	rain	six	tap/s	twelve	yourself
off	raincoat	skip/s	team	twenty	
oh	reads	sky	telephone	two	
old	red	sled	tell	umpire	